Understanding Your Two-Year-Old

Understanding Your Child Series

The Tavistock Clinic has an international reputation as a centre of excellence for training, clinical mental health work, research and scholarship. Written by professionals working in the Child and Family and the Adolescent Departments, the guides in this series present balanced and sensitive advice that will help adults to become, or to feel that they are, "good enough" parents. Each book concentrates on a key transition in a child's life from birth to adolescence, looking especially at how parents' emotions and experiences interact with those of their children. The titles in the Understanding Your Child series are essential reading for new and experienced parents, relatives, friends and carers, as well as for the multi-agency professionals who are working to support children and their families.

other titles in the series

Understanding Your Baby
Sophie Boswell
ISBN 1 84310 242 0

Understanding Your One-Year-Old
Sarah Gustavus Jones
ISBN 1 84310 241 2

Understanding Your Three-Year-Old
Louise Emanuel
ISBN 1 84310 243 9

Understanding Your Two-Year-Old

Lisa Miller

Jessica Kingsley Publishers
London and Philadelphia

First published in the United Kingdom in 2004
by Jessica Kingsley Publishers
116 Pentonville Road
London N1 9JB, England
and
400 Market Street, Suite 400
Philadelphia, PA 19106, USA

www.jkp.com

Copyright © The Tavistock Clinic 2004

Library of Congress Cataloging in Publication Data
Miller, Lisa, 1939-
Understanding your two-year-old / Lisa Miller.
   p. cm. -- (Understanding your child series)
Includes index.
ISBN 1-84310-288-9 (pbk.)
1. Toddlers. 2. Child rearing. I. Title. II. Series.
HQ774.5.M55 2004
305.232--dc22

                                                2004012455

British Library Cataloguing in Publication Data
A CIP catalogue record for this book is available from the British Library

ISBN 1 84310 2889

Printed and Bound in Great Britain by
Athenaeum Press, Gateshead, Tyne and Wear

Contents

Foreword   7

Introduction   9

1 A Sense of Self   **17**

Exploring the world – "I can do it" – The word "no" – The impulsive
two-year-old – Stability and change

2 Learning to Look After Yourself   **21**

Eating – Sleeping – Toilet-training – Pulling together these issues

3 Relationships   **29**

Mother and father – Mums and dads – A new baby – Siblings and
friends – Day-care, childminders and nannies

4 The Development of Body and Mind   **39**

Play – Books – Toys and games – Imagination and fantasy – Talking
and communication – Television and videos – The adults in the
child's world

5 The Parents   **47**

Hard work – When to worry – Difficulties in the family – Troubles
within the toddler – Complex family situations

Conclusion   53

FURTHER READING   55

HELPFUL ORGANIZATIONS   56

INDEX   59

Foreword

The Tavistock Clinic has an international reputation as a centre of excellence for training, clinical mental health work, research and scholarship. Established in 1920, its history is one of groundbreaking work. The original aim of the Clinic was to offer treatment which could be used as the basis of research into the social prevention and treatment of mental health problems, and to teach these emerging skills to other professionals. Later work turned towards the treatment of trauma, the understanding of conscious and unconscious processes in groups, as well as important and influential work in developmental psychology. Work in perinatal bereavement led to a new understanding within the medical profession of the experience of stillbirth, and of the development of new forms of support for mourning parents and families. The development in the 1950s and 1960s of a systemic model of psychotherapy, focusing on the interaction between children and parents and within families, has grown into the substantial body of theoretical knowledge and therapeutic techniques used in the Tavistock's training and research in family therapy.

The *Understanding Your Child* series has an important place in the history of the Tavistock Clinic. It has been issued in a completely new form three times: in the 1960s, the 1990s, and now, in 2004. Each time the authors, drawing on their clinical background and specialist training, have set out to reflect on the extraordinary story of "ordinary development" as it was observed and experienced at the time. Society changes, of course, and so has this series, as it attempts to make sense of everyday accounts of the ways in which a developing child interacts with his or her parents, carers and the wider world. But within this changing scene there has been something constant, and it is best described as a continuing enthusiasm for a view of development which recognizes the importance of the strong feelings and emotions experienced at each stage of development.

The context of this book is both the world of the baby and that of the one-year-old, described in the two previous volumes in this series. The author, Lisa Miller, is struck by how very young a two-year-old really is. It is true – two-year-olds certainly could not survive without a great deal of adult help. And yet, bearing in mind the previous volumes, what an enormous amount of experience, including a complex mix of emotional experiences over the first two years of life, have they already had! In a sensitive and confident way, Lisa Miller takes a view of development suffused and characterized by emotion and high feeling. In keeping with the overall approach of the series, she does not shy away from considering rage within relationships, as well as the intense feelings of frustration that are an ordinary part of the story of development. This is life as it is, rather than a more remote, romantic view of it, intolerant of conflict.

Jonathan Bradley
Child Psychotherapist
General Editor of the Understanding Your Child series

Introduction

It is sometimes hard to remember, as a parent, that someone aged two is still a very small person. The two-year-old has come a long way since birth. Looking back on the earliest days, at memories or photographs of a newborn baby, it can be hard to remember how vulnerable and totally dependent the baby was to begin with. Everything has to be done for tiny babies. Not only do we have to feed them, keep them safe and warm, clean them perseveringly and often, but we have to do their thinking for them and even some of their feeling. Babies do not know what they want; they do not recognize their own feelings; we have to interpret, guess and understand by deduction, intuition and reading the signs.

By the time the baby has arrived at two years old the picture is strikingly different. Between the ages of two and three toddlers make a substantial start on acquiring and developing the skills which will enable them to look after themselves. Already by the second birthday the toddler is entirely mobile. He or she can come and find us, run and fetch things, dash away in an elusive and inconvenient manner. Toddlers can express their own views and wishes, have minds of their own, communicate most expressively and use language with ever-increasing fluency and complexity. The whole concept of being able to clear up after themselves comes to life as with varying speeds they become toilet-trained. There is no doubt that they are separate individuals with well-developed characters, likes and dislikes, eagerness, reluctance and a push towards independence.

However, this independence is relative. As parents we can be rather seduced by the brilliance of our two-year-old's achievements. Some two-year-olds become fluent conversationalists; some turn into avid questioners; some prefer to reserve their energies for active play or for joining in with older siblings. Certainly they grow and change at speed. But in fact two-year-olds are very small people. Their own wish for independence sometimes takes us over. A father was heard saying how wonderfully resourceful his two-year-old son Robert was: Robert could open the fridge, find a box of juice, put the straw in; he could get the cheese, unwrap it, and set to eating and drinking. Indeed, this is very engaging, the two-year-old masterfully implying that he doesn't need anyone else – he can feed himself. However, we all know that really Robert is entirely dependent on the people who fill the fridge.

The human animal has a very long period of dependence; two-year-olds have little chance of surviving on their own, and just as Robert is physically dependent on the father who buys the juice and the cheese, he is psychologically dependent too. Two-year-olds need a great deal of cherishing and care. Parents are often relieved as well as a bit sad when those vulnerable earliest days are past, but it's as well to remember that the world is still a great mystery to the two-year-old. This goes for the actual world of the kitchen, the road, the park and the garden, of day-care and home; it also goes for the world of other people, who are separate and different, who have their likes and dislikes and who are not under the toddler's command. The world inside the toddler's mind is also quite a mystery to him or her – the world of thoughts, emotions, hopes, fears and desires.

There is an enormous amount for a child to discover in this third year of life. Development is proceeding at a rattling pace and the toddler's capacity to learn is breathtaking. But he or she still needs the company of an adult for much of the time both in body and in mind: the two-year-old needs protection, guidance and watchfulness as well as stimulation.

However, two-year-olds not only are interested in everything around them, but also are extremely interesting. All a short book like this can hope to do is to chime in with the natural interest people take in their children. It is possible to generalize about two-year-olds because they are all at the same stage of life. But no two are exactly alike, and it is important to remember at what different speeds children develop. Even the parent of a four-year-old can look back, as one mother did, and think what a lot of energy she put in to worrying about her son, who hardly spoke till he was two-and-a-half. She recalled how she worried about this, her neighbour worried because her son shrieked every time he saw the potty, her sister worried because her twin daughters seemed late and timid walkers: and yet, looking around now, it was clear that by the time they were about three they could all walk and talk well and were all potty trained, more or less.

The two-year-old is poised on the cusp between babyhood and childhood. Eagerly reaching out to be one of the big ones, he or she is filled with towering ambition and often can be sophisticated in understanding and achieving. But this achievement is fragile; the clever boy or girl collapses easily and we see again that we have a baby here, wanting a good deal of the same sort of intimate nurturing that the baby gets.

1

A Sense of Self

We are made up of what we were born with, or even conceived with, and that is our genetic inheritance, but just as important is what happens to us while our characters are developing. The one interacts with the other. People spend a good deal of time trying to think whether what you inherit is all important, or whether it is how you are brought up that counts. Surely it isn't a matter of one or the other – either "nature" *or* "nurture" – but the complex interplay between the two, which shapes our grown-up selves. There is no doubt that we are born unique individuals, with our own peculiar endowment and potential. But the direction in which that endowment develops, and the degree to which the potential is realized, are greatly affected by circumstances. An acorn can never grow into a tulip. But whether it grows into a mighty oak that lasts hundreds of years is related not only to its genetic make-up but also to the soil it falls in and everything that subsequently happens to it.

At two years old a very young child is clearly developing a sense of being a unique individual, a sense that "this is *me* and I do *that*". This is indeed the age when children start to use the words "I" and "me", and more important in a way than the exact words used is the meaning of them. The toddler is exploring his or her own personal world, and is beginning the long journey towards adulthood with a sense of being a person in his or her own right.

Exploring the world

The world around is a most interesting and exciting place for a two-year-old. Things that the baby of a year old passed smilingly by are now to be thought about and puzzled away at. The one-year-old is still, intellectually speaking, attached to the grown-up that he or she is with. If you give babies a telephone, they are just as likely to put it in their mouth as to imitate the adults and put it to their ear. Either way babies are content to let the adults see to the real business of telephoning. It is simply one of the many things that are beyond comprehension.

Now, for the two-year-old it's a different matter. As adults, we take for granted an innumerable number of things that we have learnt about the world. Some, like the telephone, are not only the sophisticated result of thousands of years of human endeavour, but also quite difficult to understand in their own right. How can it be that Daddy is on the phone? From the toddler's view-point, Daddy is either here, or not here. Even "not here" is still a problematic concept. What does it mean, to be somewhere else? Of course, it helps when the toddler has a picture in his mind he can refer to – "Daddy's at Grandma's house", "Daddy's at the garage" or even "Daddy's on the aeroplane". But what is he to make of the idea that "Daddy's at Grandma's, and he's on the phone to us"?

Lucy's little boy, Ned, often had to grapple with this one, since his father's work frequently took him away from the town where they lived and consequently Daddy was often on the phone. Lucy had plenty of opportunity to observe Ned's changing approach to these calls. Ned went from a puzzled delight when he first recognized that, despite some distortion, the voice coming from the telephone really sounded like Daddy. He progressed through different stages. Sometimes he seemed not only puzzled but also nervous. He rejected the phone as though it contained alarming magic. Could Daddy have got into that little black box? Ned had only just grasped the notion that Daddy could be absent and still exist. He could think of Daddy at Grandma's, which was a place they all knew well. But "in London"? What's London? And if you're in London how can you be in the phone too? Ned progressed to being able to listen to Daddy, sometimes pleased to hear him, sometimes a bit cross, as though he didn't like his father being away. But it wasn't until he was nearly three that he started having unprompted conversations with his telephone Daddy, as if it had taken him all this time to realize he could talk on the phone just like he could talk to Daddy when he's here.

Perhaps you will think I have made rather a meal of this last point, but I am trying to illustrate how complicated it is for a small child to learn about and adjust to our daily reality. There is so much to learn. But every time that something is understood and mastered there is a corresponding gain in maturity for the child. Ned could give up his belief in the telephone's magic powers – or start to – as he gradually understood how it worked and how to use it. He had the corresponding sense of being able to do things himself and a feel for himself as a person with his own powers – not magic powers, but real, true capacity.

"I can do it"

Toddlers are learning what they can and what they can't do. This is an age of extremes. Nothing is so abject as a downcast desperate toddler, and nothing so full of pure delight as an elated one. Their method of dealing with life is by taking up extreme positions, and of course they are thoroughly unbalanced as a result. Just as they are still a bit unreliable on their legs – or at least, they haven't grasped that if you run full tilt without looking where you're going you may come a cropper – they are unreliable in their feelings and reactions. They are, in fact, totally childish, even babyish, and we sometimes catch ourselves reproaching them for it.

When they can't manage something, they frequently collapse. When Sarah couldn't open the door, she flung herself on the floor weeping. When her father opened it for her, it didn't at once make things better: she'd wanted to open the door herself. She couldn't bear the idea of being shut out and nor did she like to think that Daddy could do something she couldn't. She felt small, abject and humiliated. On other occasions she would feel quite different – delighted, for example, when Daddy fetched her bike for her, feeling like a thrilled little princess as she scooted off. Her father, somewhat tired himself, had the thought, "It must be awfully tiring *being* Sarah."

Sarah could be really bossy. She seemed to want to impose her will on everyone and everything at times. This is a state of mind which by no means comes to an end with the third birthday, but it's in the two-year-old that we see it first. It's important to be able to think about why a small child so often resorts to bossiness, and to remember that it can be a defence against feeling small and weak.

Part of the toddler's extreme view of the world is bound up with the reality of his or her age and stage. Toddlers are physically very small. We only need to think that we, the grown-ups, can be around three times their height, to imagine what giants we must look. Someone only twice the height of your average adult would be well over three metres tall and look as big as a tree. We must seem alarmingly powerful, filled with knowledge, and packed with surprises.

On the one hand, it's a jolly good thing that parents are older, bigger, stronger and more experienced than children, and sometimes we can see a small child loving to be looked after, grateful for somebody who'll take over and sort things out, deeply relishing a hug, a kiss and a bit of babying. Sarah, who was capable and lively, was also highly strung and prone to collapse. It was as though at day-nursery she had to will herself on to ever greater efforts, speeding around, on the run from feelings of being unsure or little. When she got home she was frequently in a bad mood, ordering her father about, refusing to eat and finally having a full-blown tantrum. Her father, who was the one who picked her up and took her home, came to see that she was completely exhausted by the effort she was making to keep herself together and pretend she was big. Her idea of being big was based on a little child's idea of being a huge, all-powerful person.

It was fortunate that her father wasn't a giant, but just an ordinary grown-up person, much bigger than Sarah, who could take over and see that what she needed was a soothing and cosy approach. She didn't need excitement, she didn't need distraction; she did need a quiet time and some undivided attention. Otherwise matters could get worse and it could be impossible to get her to eat her tea, have her bath and go to bed, for in such a state of mind her favourite word was "no", which she would utter with extreme passion and resolution.

The word "no"

Two-year-olds begin to find the force of the word "no". In a way this is good. We don't want our children to grow up without being able to assert themselves or to refuse what is bad for them. The problem is that toddlers are at the very start of growing up. They often quite literally don't know what's good for them. They are only now becoming aware of their powers. Whereas babies can make their likes and dislikes known and have considerable ability to refuse to do what they don't want to do, it is only now that with a growing sense of self, the toddler starts to see and feel that he or she can say "No".

To begin with, two-year olds are like people in charge of a big crude machine. They lack subtlety. If something looks nasty they may refuse it with all their energy, never mind that last time they accepted it eagerly. They do however need, at least sometimes, to be treated with the thoughtfulness which they themselves cannot achieve. It can be almost automatic – more than just tempting – to fall into the toddler's own mode and join battle. This is an eyeball-to-eyeball battle where, because you are bigger, you may be able to force a victory, but where you feel afterwards that nothing much was resolved.

Of course, there are times when it is simply not possible to do anything except take charge. A mother, Deb, took her youngest, Alex, to work for a bit. Alex had a lovely time but got over-excited at the end and ran about among the desks, having had lots of thrilling attention. Deb saw that it was time to finish and go home, and she caught up Alex, who at once began to squall. Paying the minimal attention, she said "Come on, Alex," and calling out goodbye, she carried him off. Through Alex's noisy objections, she heard the voice of a rather admiring male colleague calling out, "You certainly breed them tough-minded, Deb." Alex yelled his way down the stairs; Deb spoke to him sympathetically, strapped him in his car seat and as she drove off saw his thumb go in his mouth and his head nod. Next day, without Alex, she went to the office where the same colleague said to her, "He fought you to a draw, I see." Deb smiled. It seemed as though the colleague had felt that neither side was crushed.

Maybe this is a point to consider. When we join battle with a toddler there is a huge difference between taking over, as Deb did with Alex, and knowing within ourselves that we have "lost it" or "gone over the top", really become deeply angry and stirred and not able to rein that in. There must be very few parents who do not have the experience of feeling guilty and regretful because they know they have lost their tempers and gone too far. The raw nature of the toddler's feelings can set fire to something in us which is almost equally primitive. It can be a struggle to manage one's own feelings, to say "No" to oneself, to recall how very big and potentially frightening one is.

The difficult lesson for young children to take in is that "no" can be a good and vital word. At least, it seems to them that it's an excellent word when they say it, but horribly unwelcome when it's said to them. Perhaps we can sympathize. But it's very important that we get in our bones a feeling of when it's right and necessary to say "No" to ourselves. Many examples of this are trivial, but they all mount up; there are times when grown-ups say "No" in quite a nice way, and they are right to do so. At this stage the world is full of dangers, big and small, for a two-year-old, and the word "no" has to be backed up with actions and precautions. It's no good *only* saying "No" to a toddler about hot pans, fires, matches, irons: these need to be on the back burner, behind a guard, out of reach. But we also need to explain. Sometimes a child seems so intelligent and sensible it looks as though explanation is enough. Don't believe it. Deb got home to find a frantic nanny and Alex displaying with shy pride a professionally bandaged paw. He had touched the iron.

The impulsive two-year-old

As with Alex, a two-year-old's self-control is not to be trusted. The sense of being in command of oneself, of learning from past experience, is hard won. Most parents understand that, just as a small child's feelings swing between extremes, their impulses are similarly unsteady and they can act upon them in a split second. "Oh help, have scissors, must cut," gasped a horrified visiting mother when her little Sophie in a trice cut a gash in the curtain.

All this is part of grappling with reality, getting to know not only the world outside, but also the world inside yourself. The two-year-old child, like Sophie, is not able to think ahead, or indeed to think about either the consequences of her action or what the reasons for it might be. Acquiring these capacities are linked to acquiring a sense of time – of the past from which you draw conclusions and learn, and of the future which you become able to envisage.

Tiny babies have no sense of time. Parents get hooked in to this and a week can seem an age. Two-year-olds often give evidence of wonderful memories, but these memories are not as yet reliable places, banks to be drawn upon at will. Most people's conscious memories, a sense of continuous existence, start around four. We may have the odd intermittent flash of memory from a time before that, but it isn't the same. What we have to do for tiny children is to act as supplementary memories; we hold on to the continuity of their life for them. Without even thinking, we remind them of other times when something like this happened; we teach them ways of measuring time: we'll do it "when the big ones come home from school", "after you've been to nursery", "in the morning".

Two-year-olds need adult minds to help them extract order and sense from what might otherwise be the confusion of existence. They also need lives that are to some degree predictable. Routine is their friend: not, of course, a stultifying mindless routine, but something in the shape of their day that gives security in a bewildering world. Sarah, the little girl who used to be in such a state of upset sometimes when she got home, came to love her home-time evening routine dearly. Though she was in a good day-care set-up, there was patently much she found challenging about it. She liked very much to insist on the same activity every teatime: a story from a book while she ate, a little game with Daddy after that, a soothing video while Daddy got on with cooking and waited for Mummy to get home. Then Mummy would be with her, talk to her and give her a bath. The pattern of bath and bed was always the same: Sarah insisted on it. She derived a great deal of comfort from the constancy of the setting, a routine which she could relax into, and in combination with this the close and affectionate attention from Daddy and Mummy. This does not mean that every evening went smooth as clockwork. Sarah was herself; she needed her parents to deal with all her different aspects. She could be sweet, trusting, agreeable; she could be quarrelsome, angry, and stubborn. But this was against a stable evening background which she plainly enjoyed and which her parents strove to provide.

Stability and change

The two-year-old, tossed about inwardly by all sorts of contradictions and impulses, needs such stability as we can provide. When a family goes through a period of instability the effect on a toddler is usually marked. Things are changing quickly enough anyway for ever-developing toddlers, and they often react quite strongly to changes in the family. Sometimes it is hard to recognize that this is what is happening.

It is not at all unusual for parents to be worried about their small children without realizing that they are affected by wider family happenings. This is partly because two-year-olds themselves do not know what is the matter. Doctors, health visitors and other professionals are familiar with parents who are concerned because their toddler has suddenly begun to refuse food, or wake up at night, or to display miserable, anxious, clingy behaviour. Professionals have often had the experience of asking what's going on in the family's life and discovering that some upheaval is at hand. Maybe there is a house move, a new baby, a divorce, a bereavement – and the two-year-old is acting in response to a general feeling of disorder and instability. It's usually quite a relief to the parent to discover some reason for disturbance and a reminder that two-year-olds can't as yet think over and understand what's happening; they just react.

2

Learning to Look After Yourself

Learning to look after yourself is only just beginning for a two-year-old, but it is a process that already has a history. Some of the concerns that loom largest in parents' minds are those that connect with our primary needs, which have existed since birth. The new baby must eat, sleep, be cleaned, bathed and changed. These needs must be satisfied in some way all our lives long, and they all link with ways in which two-year-olds are learning gradually to look after their own needs.

Eating

Feeding a new baby is something in which the grown-up plays a major part. But by the time that babies are two, they have progressed to the state where they pick up their own piece of bread, drink from their own cup and even wield a spoon. What does this mean both to the toddler and to the parent?

Eating is full of significance: we must eat to stay alive. There is nothing like a baby or a toddler with a good appetite to make a mother feel cheerful and optimistic. Here, it seems, is a child with an appetite for life, who appreciates what's on offer, who reassures Mummy that she's doing a good job. No need to worry. What is more, we acknowledge that eating – taking in food – is a kind of prototype for other sorts of taking in: we talk about being thirsty for information, or hungry for knowledge. We are aware that the feeding baby is taking in more than milk: the baby is taking in attention and affection, and taking in something about the person who feeds him or her. Eventually babies grab the spoon to feed themselves, having absorbed the idea of a person who does the feeding, and two-year-olds are now in a position to feed themselves.

By now body and mind are a little more distinct from each other. All sorts of complexities are clear in the two-year-old's attitude towards food. Parents are very lucky indeed if they get a clear run through infancy and the early years with a child whose appetite seldom fails. This is often an area of anxiety and difficulty. We all would like our children to eat up with happy relish, but many have patches of not doing so, and some seem quite clearly to have times when they've got their wires crossed – the delicious food, made with care, necessary for existence, looks off-putting instead of inviting.

Mothers are particularly sensitive to the effect of a small child refusing food. Perhaps an experienced mother with a child who normally eats well can be cheerful and philosophical about a toddler who behaves as though he has been offered poison. But many mothers feel hurt: doesn't the child trust me or like me? They feel anxious: is he going to starve? And then they feel angry. None of these are feelings they wish to have.

All this shows what strenuous demands toddlers can make on their carers, when even a simple meal can turn into an emotional battleground. This is partly because a two-year-old needs a parent to be very receptive to his or her feelings. But he or she also needs a parent who can manage to hang on to being an adult. The area of eating strikes such deep and primitive chords in us all that we do sometimes have to struggle to hold on to our adult, sensible selves, the selves who know that one missed meal, or more, will not bring about starvation or even malnourishment; that children have passing fancies; broccoli is poison to one child and delightful to another.

Kate took her two-year-old son, Sam, to have lunch with her new friend, Nora, and Nora's three small boys. Kate was slightly dreading it. She was quite sure that Nora's children ate absolutely anything and she was well acquainted with Sam's rather restricted tastes in food. Indeed, that was putting it mildly. What on earth might Nora expect him to eat? He wouldn't touch tomatoes, beans, peas, cabbage... The list seemed endless. But oh joy, Nora produced by chance a menu acceptable to Sam and turning to Kate she said, "How on earth d'you get him to eat broccoli like that? It's sensational!"

Sometimes we get an insight into the imaginings of a small child which may be throwing a powerful colouring over his or her actions. The same Sam nearly a year later, about to turn three, was still choosy and a less than hearty eater. His granny had produced sausages for lunch. She cut a piece off and offered it to Sam, who looked at it dubiously. "Does the sausage *want* to be eaten?" he enquired. In this case, reflected Kate to herself, it was probably a good thing that it was granny who was fielding the question. Granny replied with complete conviction, "Oh yes of course, that's what sausages are *for*," and in it went. Kate thought to herself that she could have got a bit hung up on Sam's doubts, sympathized with his sensitivities, and answered a bit more equivocally. Sam did indeed occasionally look at his food as though he were worried about it or even frightened by it.

This relates to the way a small child inhabits a different world from the adult. We, for example, take it for granted that living things are quite different from inanimate ones, that a sausage does not have feelings, thoughts and wishes like a person. Two-year-olds do not grasp this, and all kinds of activities (not only eating) take place for them in a world that is different from ours. From time to time we get a glimpse of how things look to them, and this helps us to remain sympathetic.

Sleeping

Another area that can try a parent's patience severely is that of sleep: like failure to eat, failure to sleep arouses in us a problematical cocktail of emotional response – anxiety and anger in particular.

Failure to sleep takes several forms. There is the child who won't go to sleep in her own bed, but who wants to fall asleep on a sofa and be moved when asleep; the child who insists that a parent stays with him till he is overcome by sleep; the one who calls the parent back every two minutes; the one who reappears downstairs repeatedly; the one who wakes every couple of hours in the night; and probably a great many other variations on similar themes. What do these different sorts of sleeping difficulties have in common? Perhaps with all of them there is an underlying problem for the child in being separate, or rather in fully realizing that they are separate beings from their mum or dad.

If you lie by yourself in your cot or your bed, and wait for sleep to come, you run the risk of occasionally feeling alone, or even lonely. This is one of the prices that we pay for becoming independent beings: we have to develop the capacity for being alone. Or, if you wake up in the night, not only might you feel alone, but also you might have to wonder where Daddy and Mummy are. Have they gone away? Perhaps they're doing something together and you're left out? Probably all children wake in the night: the difference is between times when they wake up and feel quite secure and happy in the feeling that

Daddy and Mummy are downstairs or in the next room, and times when they wake and feel lonely or frightened, prey to fears and imaginings, which they can't cope with alone.

Ordinarily these times (of being woken, say, by a bad dream) are fairly few and far between. But for some children it is hard to develop some tolerance for even the milder feelings of loneliness or anxiety. Of course, if they never go to sleep alone, they never get any practice in feeling alone, nor practice in managing those feelings.

A little girl called Frances had always shared her parents' bed. Although they had made some efforts to get her to sleep in her cot, she had resisted them. By the time she was two her parents were rather fed up with having no time or space or privacy for themselves. However, Frances seemed to fall into such a panic whenever her own room (prettily furnished and inviting) was mentioned as a place to sleep that they would always give way. But gradually they began to see it as a problem that needed attention and discussion, rather than a situation which would naturally and easily resolve itself without any particular effort from them.

When they started to talk about it seriously they realized two things. First, they were not the only ones deprived of a separate existence. Frances, too, had no space of her own. She was in a sense deprived as well. Second, they began to link the night-time situation with daytime ones where Frances found it hard to say goodbye. The conclusion they gradually came to was that Frances was becoming a bit of a tyrant. Could that be good for her?

When they presented a united front and explained to Frances that she was going to start sleeping in her own bed, they had a very cross little girl to deal with. But their shared conviction that the time had come clearly made itself known to her. They began to see that they, two grown-ups, had been quite frightened at the idea Frances would get cross, and worried that they might get angry with her.

Two-year-olds can spark off intense feelings of anger in us. Frances's parents could, as it happened, help each other to tolerate their feelings of irritation and helplessness and yet remain firm. In this case it took only a short time for Frances to accept that time had moved on, she was a big girl now and the proper place for her was out of Mummy and Daddy's bed.

Sometimes there can be reasons in the parents, rather than in the children, for some sleeping difficulties. Two people were watching a television programme about children with sleeping difficulties. A family – mother, father and a small boy called Peter – had volunteered to follow a psychologist's plan to deal with Peter's repeated refusal to go and stay in his bed. The mother was instructed to put him back every time he woke up and to stay outside his room, but always to return him to his bed. The camera followed the family and the process. It was all rather painful and protracted, but eventually Peter was sleeping and staying in his room. One of the people watching the programme turned to the other and said, "I wonder how those two parents will get on now they've got time to themselves." Almost at once, as the credits rolled, a voice over said, "Sadly, after the completion of this film Sandra and Jimmy's marriage broke up and they parted." Clearly, the viewer's hunch was correct. Peter's presence, and the previous horrid rows they had been having with him, had taken the place of mutual disagreements which surfaced once Peter was no longer the focus of conflict.

Toilet-training

Toilet-training is another classical area of worry and conflict. Sometimes people say, "Why worry yourself about toilet-training in these days of wonderful disposable nappies? Surely the child will train itself in time." Alas, though some children may "train themselves", by no means all of them will. It is tempting to think that all troubles over toilet-training came in the past from injudiciously early or punitive attempts to enforce it. Unfortunately this turns out not to be so. There is no automatically simple way of training a child to use the potty.

There is no doubt about it, some children are much easier than others. Thomas had just turned two. He was the youngest child. His dad said to his mum, "Isn't it about time that child was trained?" His mum, hard-pressed, running a family and a job, gave a furious yelp, "Why don't you do it if you think it's so important?" "OK," said his dad defiantly, "I will then." The dad solemnly explained to Thomas that he wasn't going to wear a nappy any more, that he was going to sit on the potty or go to the loo like the big ones and that this weekend he, Daddy, was personally going to see to it. Thomas, who wasn't a great talker, looked serious and owlish. One might have expected it not to work at all. But it did. Much to his mum's amazement and amusement, Thomas took to being trained like a duck to water, carrying on after the weekend with his childminder, and reaching even greater heights when within a remarkably short space of time he also stopped wetting his night nappy and left it off.

Of course, they were all lucky. Clearly the rather silent Thomas had an ambitious streak after all. Irritable though mum felt initially, she was actually on good and loving terms with dad. Eccentric though dad's approach might appear, he was actually very kind as well as determined.

Many people however feel that they are unlucky over toilet-training. It is a situation that seems made for conflict. The small child begins at about 18 months to be interested in the idea of distinguishing rubbish – what you throw away – from valuable stuff that you keep. The trouble is, when parents start toilet-training children round about two, there are two particular difficulties that kick in. The first is a mulish determination that poos and wees are special and precious and don't want to be thrown away. This is a hanging on to the baby's lack of discrimination – the baby has no sense of disgust, no feeling there's anything undesirable about poo. The toddler is definitely acquiring discrimination, but sometimes with reluctance. The second difficulty is that reluctance is a very two-year-old attribute. Two-year-olds are just beginning to realize that they can flex their muscles, refuse, disagree. If they don't want to, they won't.

So all kinds of things can become battles. Parents realize, sometimes with a shock, that they can't *make* a child do something instantly. Your powers to force a child to eat, sleep and wee in the potty at command are severely limited, especially when you rightly shrink from coercion. On the one hand we have a child's wish to please his or her parents, to have that lovely glow that comes from feeling you're a good, clever person and have made Mummy or Daddy happy. We also have the thrust towards development, the child's interest in growing and developing, the wish to do new things and the gratifications of laudable ambition. On the contrary we have all the negativistic feelings – the "I don't *want* to!" and "I won't!" – and the huge feelings of "No!" that can engulf the two-year-old in us all. There are also anxieties that surround toilet-training. Just as children can have fantasies about food, or imaginings about the dark, they can and frequently do invest the contents of their body with all sorts of imagined significance. Some children are not at all sure that poos are rubbish: how are they different from other parts of their bodies? Do they really want to push them out? Worse still, send them down that alarming loo? It's worth noticing how long children like playing with pooey-looking substances (mud pies, wet sand, thick paint) as if it's with much reluctance we give up the idea of poos being rather wonderful, even magic.

Pulling together these issues

What have these issues (eating, sleeping, toilet-training) got in common? They are all potential areas of anxiety in the life of the two-year-old. Perhaps it is because they all relate to the central point about development at this age: this is an age where some crucial facts about separation and loss have to be faced in order for the development of independence and a sense of self to proceed. Being able to feed yourself, face going into the dark on your own, take charge of your own toileting, all are points of growth. You have to say goodbye to the life of the dependent baby, a life where you were fed, rocked to sleep, your nappy changed, and take to the life of the pre-school child with its approach to the world of bigger children.

Two-year-olds cannot think of these things, but they can sense they are at a time of great change. Change always brings turbulence, and being two is being at a turbulent stage where toddlers are pulled back and forth inside themselves – back to babyhood, on to childhood.

Parents are not always quite sure what support to offer in the face of what people like to call "the terrible twos". Not all two-year-olds are terrible by any means, but perhaps the phrase comes partly from our instinctive understanding that for the child it can be a hard time. We have our more adult perspective to offer: we can, when we're on good form, see that all these troubles pass and that children grow up quickly. On the basis of this, and all sorts of sensible reminders to ourselves, we can't magically make things all right, but we can keep children company when they are miserable and act as a persevering support to the bit of the child that actually *wants* to feed him- or herself and be able to stand on their own two feet. This doesn't involve denying that being two and looking after a two-year-old are both hard work. The intimacy involved means that we feel for and with our young children and sometimes have ourselves to struggle to separate our thinking selves from our empathy with the toddler.

Tracey had two girls and the elder one had been easy enough to wean from the bottle: she had given it up finally at about 14 months with no more than a hint. But Jessica was a different matter. At two she was still demanding milk from a bottle. If Tracey tried to give her a cup when she didn't want a cup, Jessica would howl, refuse the drink, run away and dig her head in the sofa with her bottom up in the air and her legs kicking. Tracey and Mark, her partner, found themselves increasingly uncomfortable about yielding to blackmail – the implied threat that if Jessica didn't get her bottle, she would never drink again and the world would come to an end. Tracey made up her mind that she would have to persevere, as Jessica's third birthday approached. It took nearly a fortnight, where often Jessica drank less than Tracey thought she should, but Tracey was inwardly determined (though sometimes worried). She managed to keep calm, remind Jessica that she could drink fine from a cup, and in the end to everyone's relief Jessica finally seemed to realize that her life didn't depend on the bottle. It was a definite step forward, even in Jessica's own mind. Perhaps Jessica had had the chance to take in the idea of a mum who could be resolute but not unkind, and perhaps this idea would become part of Jessica's own character and internalized sense of relationship.

3

Relationships

This chapter examines the importance to the two-year-old of relationships with all the people in his or her life.

Mother and father

For every child there is a sense in which the parents are the most important people in his or her life. Two concurrent questions arise: who made me? And who brought me up? Two-year-olds are at the start of formulating these questions, which are fundamental to us all in the establishment of our identity, our sense of who we are. Our genetic inheritance depends upon the two people who, one way or another, came together to create us. The influences brought to bear upon us from the times of conception and birth are directly related to the people who have taken care of us and exerted their influence upon us in the context of accepting responsibility for our dependent selves.

Children have often been raised by people who are not their parents – grandparents, a couple of maiden aunts, adoptive parents, an elder sibling – and yet the question of our biological parents remains a central one to us all. We have in our minds the *idea* of our parents, in the world of memory, imagination and dreams, in the world of our thoughts both conscious and unconscious, at the back and the front of our minds, above the surface and below. The idea of our parents is a most influential one. If, for example, we do not know who our father is, we form the idea of a father built up from all our experiences of relationships with both men and women, our experiences in life, in film, theatre, television and books. Equally, if someone other than our biological mother takes on the work of nurturing us, we form the idea of a mother from this person and all our varied and complex other relationships and experiences.

We also form the idea of a connection between mother and father, one which, essentially, produced us.

It is probably easiest to see how important both father and mother are by observing a two-year-old who lives with them both, and for whom the future questions "Who made me?" and "Who brought me up?" can be straightforwardly answered. However, we see *all* two-year-olds in the process of building up an idea of mother and father. It is painful for some people to contemplate the idea that both parents are important, but we have to acknowledge the truth: there is no such thing as a fatherless child.

Mums and dads

The two-year-old is still most definitely attached to his or her mother. Mum is the person you run back to at once if you feel the slightest threat or concern. If she isn't there, you run to the most mummyish person present, the person who reminds you most of your mum, the person who corresponds with your idea of Mummy. She is the object of passionate attachment, the person the toddler depends upon, admires and loves above anything. But wait! There's a complication. There's somebody else who the toddler also depends upon, admires and loves: his or her dad. It's fine if you can love them both at once, but what if you start perceiving their rival claims? What if you start trying to be attached to two separate people at once? How do you manage the question of divided loyalties?

In one form or another this problem has to be faced. This is because not only does the toddler become aware of the attraction of someone else besides mum, but also he or she becomes aware that Mummy herself has time for somebody else. Here we have an emotional crux, a situation that must be struggled with and surmounted if emotional development is to continue unhindered. Part of the small boy or girl wants to cling to the idea that he or she has an exclusive relationship with Mummy: there are just the two of them, and that's that. Chloe would hardly allow even her uncle to speak to his own sister, Chloe's mum, at one point. "Go away!" she would cry, clinging to her mother, "Don't talk!"

Of course, at other times it may be dad who exerts the pull. The little boy who has clung to his mum, who wants to get into bed on her side and cuddle her and push Daddy away, is the same little boy who immensely admires his dad, longs to drive the car or use the computer or do whatever he thinks it is that Daddy does. There is a conflict here which will take some time to resolve. How can you love two people at once?

And how can you allow those two to have a relationship with each other which excludes you? This recalls the little girl called Frances referred to in Chapter 2, who found such difficulty in being on her own while her parents were together. Yet children have to allow their parents – separately and together – to have some freedom. When you are two years old, this is hard. You find it difficult to imagine that Mummy is going off somewhere else without you. Worse, that there might be times when she would prefer to be without you, or prefer somebody or something else. This takes years to come to terms with, and the two-year-old is only at the start of it. We instinctively like to let our toddlers down lightly, to reassure them by word and action that they are still central people in our world. Only gradually does reality creep in: there is another woman in Daddy's life, and it's Mummy. Mummy *does* feel the need for someone else's company – Daddy's. Even if there aren't second parents around, there may well be rivals: there is no way round it.

A new baby

This brings us to the question of a new baby – proof positive, in one sense, that something has been going on behind the toddler's back. I am not suggesting that a two-year-old consciously knows how a baby is conceived; on the other hand, there is no question that something has happened to produce a little rival.

A common time for people to have another baby is when the first child is about two. It looks reasonable: the elder is no longer a baby, but the pair of them will be near enough in age for them to be companionable. This is true, but there is quite a long way to go before they can really be friends and play-mates.

Both boys and girls are intensely interested in pregnancy. Simon, aged two-and-a-half, was seen sticking out his tummy as hard as he could. When he was asked what he was doing, he said he had a baby in his tummy. After hearing him say this several times, his mum mildly remarked that he was a boy, and when he grows up he'd be a daddy, and daddies don't have babies. Simon was very cross and claimed vigorously that he *would* have a baby, he'd be a mummy. His conviction was so emphatic that his mum thought she'd better let well alone for the time being. Simon admired and envied his mother's wonderful capacity to have a baby inside and couldn't bear the idea that it wasn't possible for him. For Daisy, of course, it would be possible. But it seemed to make her thoroughly cross and difficult: rather than straightforwardly claiming to have babies inside herself, she wouldn't do what her mum said, refused to sit at the table, put on her Wellington boots, get off the swing. It was as though she were resentful of her mum's superior capacities; she was constantly interfering with her mum's mothering powers. It was very tiring. It made her mother annoyed and put her on edge. From time to time, however, Daisy would collapse in sobs, as though she were both sorry about being a nuisance and frightened at angering her mother.

In both these cases it was a good thing that there were fathers about. Simon's dad paid Simon some extra attention and, without realizing it himself, made Simon feel that dads were pretty important and interesting too – not such a bad thing to grow up to be. Daisy's father gave her mum a much-needed break, taking Daisy out and also providing that bit of extra care. Daisy began to feel a little better, as though Mummy hadn't got all the goodies – it wasn't quite so bad just to be a little girl.

When the two new babies arrived, Simon and Daisy both had mixed reactions. It's rather important to look out for this, and to realize that the birth of a new baby inspires two contrary sorts of feelings in the elder child. First, there are positive feelings. It really is nice to have a new brother or sister. Even very small children can feel proud and tender as they see a tiny newborn. These feelings are helped by identifying with proud and loving parents, and also by identifying with being a loved and wanted baby – in effect, having a memory of what it's like to be a cherished infant. Second, there are difficult feelings. Older children cannot avoid some sense of being replaced and pushed out. Some parents can even remember what it was like: one father said, "I couldn't think why my parents kept on having more babies when they'd got ME!" Everyone's attention is at times on the newcomer, and indeed, so long as this isn't overdone, it has to be: it's no good neglecting either child at the expense of the other.

What is hard for two-year-olds is struggling with these contrary feelings when they aren't much more than babies themselves. They need a good deal of help and warmth. What really doesn't help is when parents ignore the mixed quality of the toddler's feelings. Sometimes one hears how much the toddler adores the new baby, even when an observer can see obvious signs of something quite different. Ben's mother told a visitor that Ben was simply wonderful with the baby, but as soon as his mum left the room, Ben, with a sidelong glance at the visitor, moved to the sofa with the clear intention of tipping Ruby off it. The visitor sprang up, Ben retreated, and the smiling mother returned, congratulating Ben once more on his goodness. There is a bit of a problem here. Ben feels that he has to attack Ruby secretly, as though he is worried his mother couldn't bear it if she saw how jealous he was. Yet he does seem to hope for some adult help: he definitely looks at the visitor, drawing her attention to what he feels so tempted to do. With any luck Ben's hostility may come out and be recognized without too much shock and horror. It would be a pity if it had to go underground and run the risk of spoiling the relationship between him and Ruby. Ruby needs protecting from Ben, but Ben also needs protecting from his unmanageable hostile urges. He can't quite do it alone.

Ignoring jealousy and hostility is clearly not helpful, but doing things the other way round isn't either. Daisy, the little girl who had been difficult during her mother's pregnancy, continued to be difficult after her new sister's birth. She poured her milk on the floor, screamed and woke the baby, and refused to be helpful. Daisy's mother felt overwhelmed. All she could see in Daisy was a jealous child: she constantly discussed Daisy's problem with her friends and family. One of these friends happened to notice how miserable Daisy looked, and couldn't help wondering whether Daisy was being given a fair chance to be nicer. Her mum seemed to have got so depressed and con-vinced that Daisy would never get on with Annie. Once more, over time it was Daisy's father who came to the rescue, observing that Daisy had complicated reactions to Annie's birth which included a fair measure of covert interest in the baby. The side of her which was indeed interested in having a sister was able to emerge over time.

What Daisy found hard to believe was that there was room for two little girls in her parents' minds. This is a more troublesome concept for a small child than one might think. The idea that the toddler is all-in-all to his or her adored parents is one that is given up only reluctantly. It is hard enough for small children to imagine that their mum and dad get together in their absence – to think that mum can love both dad and toddler, or that dad can do likewise. But once the child can imagine, or discover by experience, that Mummy and Daddy really can look after two children – that rival demands can be accommodated, that the conflict between love and hate can be managed, that the toddler is still loved but the baby isn't deprived either – then the toddlers' confidence in their parents is vastly increased and their horizons expand correspondingly.

Siblings and friends

Not all two-year-olds have younger siblings, of course; some may be the middle child or the youngest. Sibling relationships are central to how we form relationships with our peers: school classmates, workmates, neighbours, colleagues and adult friends. The capacity to form friendly relationships with people has early roots and we shall turn to actual friendships in a minute. The idea of helpful, cooperative, friendly relations is first absorbed from our parents' relationship with each other and with ourselves from the earliest days. Children who are brought up in an atmosphere of constant violent rows and abuse between parents will certainly have difficulty getting on with people their own age. We learn about compromise, negotiation, working together, quarrelling and making up, consideration and forgiveness from our experiences in early years.

It is easy to see how this happens when there is more than one child in the family. How does an only child learn about sibling relationships? Perhaps it is important to remember that brothers and sisters, like mothers and fathers, are at root a powerful *idea*, as well as in some cases a fact. Children brought up by people who are not their parents still have an idea, very influential to their emotional development, of mother and father. Similarly, only children develop the *idea* of brothers and sisters to whom they relate, an idea built from a combination of imagination, fantasy and experience. As common sense suggests, it is essential that the only child has experience of the give-and-take, the rivalries, pleasures and problems that arise from a close constant link with people his or her own age.

Nathan was an only child and his parents did not plan to have any more. They felt regretful and a little guilty about this. Nathan's mother, however, was determined to make the most of a family living nearby; the parents all met and got on well, and in this other family there were three children. When Nathan was two he and his mum began regular activities with the other children and their mother. To begin with, Nathan was rather bewildered, and would hang on to his mother despite the fact that the other three children were quite welcoming. His mother became inwardly anxious and rather ashamed – "What a wimp!" she thought. Checking herself, she tried to think how few children of his own age Nathan had met – older ones, yes, but not ones round his own age. Perhaps it wasn't so odd that he felt nervous. Partly because she herself struck up a lively friendship with the other mum, and began to value the mutual visiting for her own sake as well as Nathan's, she persevered. Both families were rewarded by the interchange: all the children became fond of Nathan and he of them, and his mother observed a good while later that, even though Nathan had gone to nursery now, he still regarded these three children as his own special friends.

Perhaps this sounds rather too optimistic. Brothers and sisters are not always known for getting on well together. It's important to recall, when we're dealing with pre-school children, that small children are not in command of themselves; they need adult supervision, protection and thought. We all have a latent bully in ourselves somewhere, who can, especially if we are small, be roused. Two-year-olds sometimes need protecting from older children, just as baby Ruby needed to be protected from her elder brother Ben's uncontrollable urge to push her off the sofa and back where she came from. Neither the bully nor the victim gains from any failure in the grown-ups to take the responsibility.

In the natural quest for friends for Nathan, his parents were pleased to think how many of their own friends had children around Nathan's age so that family friendships could be established. One such family included a little boy, Danny, who was about four years old. Nathan's parents thought that it would be lovely for Nathan to play with a boy a bit older, but it became gradually clear that this might be a problem. Danny's parents had had upheavals in their marriage, and Nathan's parents appreciated that this would affect Danny. However, they were disturbed when they saw Danny's behaviour towards Nathan. Danny had outwardly toughened up; he insisted (said his mother) on having very short big-boy hair and big-man boots, and he raced about, ordering Nathan around and shouting or shoving when Nathan didn't come up to scratch. Nathan found this frightening. Over the months, Nathan's parents grew more worried as they saw no sign of this abating. Danny's parents would scold him and reprove him, but all that this seemed to achieve over time was to make Danny secretive. He would go off into the garden with Nathan, and Nathan would come in crying.

After a good deal of heart-searching Nathan's parents decided that this couldn't go on. Perhaps it would have been better to talk it over with Danny's parents, but they didn't feel it was possible. The only solution was to find ways to see that Danny and Nathan weren't alone together. Although Nathan's parents felt certain they must put Nathan's needs first, they could also see that Danny was in real trouble, which wasn't helped by his putting in a lot of practice in bullying the sensitive Nathan. We might think that Nathan's vulnerability reminded Danny of his sensitive side, which was bewildered, panicky and wounded when his parents' troubles impinged on him. In attacking Nathan, Danny was trying to quell his own vulnerability.

But of course, Nathan was a real child, really suffering. The interchanges were bad for him, damaging his faith in friendliness and cooperation, and giving him an unhelpful taste of taking the victim position. Nathan's other choice, if he didn't want to be victim, was to gang up with Danny. It was when his parents saw this happening – Nathan copying Danny, racing round with him, eagerly talking about killing – that they decided enough was enough.

It is worth remembering that bullies are themselves in trouble; with small children this situation can be remedied in a way that it can't when the child is a teenager. Bullying can go on among siblings, of course, and it becomes a matter of serious concern where a pattern becomes fixed over time.

With two-year-olds we can't think of their aggression as being as formed as it had become in poor Danny. Jessica's mother took her to the sandpit, where a younger child sweetly meandered up and helped herself to Jessica's bucket. Quick as a wink, Jessica turned round and bopped the child on the head with her plastic spade. Jessica's mum, Tracey, leapt up in horror. Could this be Jessica? Jessica, who got along so nicely with her boy cousins and was so robust and cheerful if her elder sister was demanding? The younger child wailed, Tracey had to apologize and tell Jessica she mustn't do that again. But, guess what, Jessica seemed to be in for a run of it. After a few similar skirmishes it died down again – but not before Tracey had had to rethink her picture of Jessica slightly. She realized that her image of Jessica needed adjusting to include the fact that Jessica could be just as impatient as her elder sister. Jessica was seen as a determined, cheerful child, good at fitting in with her elders, but her mum now saw that she had her own feelings towards youthful rivals. This Jessica was the same one who had difficulty in giving up her bottle. It looks as though she found the position of youngest quite comfortable and didn't brook rivals easily.

At another level, one has to remember that Jessica, like all two-year-olds, had a large lesson to begin to learn, a lesson that we need to relearn all our lives to some degree. This involves understanding that *all* other people are individuals just as we are, with feelings, thoughts, susceptibilities, hopes and fears. The two-year-old is just starting to have empathy and concern for others. This cannot fully be felt until, as now, a child starts to be aware that the other person is a separate person with their own life. When Jessica hit the toddling child, Jessica was at that moment aware of the child only as a nuisance to be got rid of. She had no possible powers of thinking, "What would I feel like if someone did that to me?" Actually, we also know that Jessica had a history of *not* minding if one of her boy cousins or her sister took her things: she was famous for good-temperedly finding something else. Had she been avoiding feeling upset herself? And was she now, at two-and-a-half, beginning rather reluctantly to find that she *had* to think about people feeling a bit bruised?

It is interesting to note that Jessica's series of sharpish attacks on younger children was eventually succeeded by a period where she became particularly attentive to small creatures – pets, dolls, babies in prams. Her parents had by no means been mistaken in thinking she was a good-natured child. But she was a human being, and like the rest of us she had good and bad sides, and was helped by her parents recognizing this.

Day-care, childminders and nannies

We have seen how the two-year-old is becoming a sociable creature. Parents make their own choices about how their children are looked after, and usually feel that the choice they are making is a serious one, making allowance for the needs of everyone in the family. It is not easy to make these choices. We are aware nowadays of the importance of early experience in building the future adult, so there is bound to be some anxiety concerning who looks after our children.

This is not the place to discuss the question generally, but perhaps some brief thoughts about the two-year-old's care are in order. What are the two-year-old's needs? What are the advantages of different kinds of care?

The advantages of day-care at some kind of organized nursery – either part-time or full-time – are obvious. Parents are spared the problems associated with having just one person (childminder or nanny) looking after the child: the main problem is unreliability. If you *have* to be at a job, it is sickening news if the childminder has injured her back or the nanny is leaving. However, parents who choose one person to do the job do so usually in the belief that two-year-olds need to be able to make a real relationship with the person to whom their care is confided. It is important to establish that in a day-care situation there is enough conscientious adult attention to go round. Not only do children's physical well-being and safety depend on the presence of an adult who is interested enough to be really observant, but also their psychological development depends on something similar. The two-year-old needs to be accompanied by a thinking adult mind for a good portion of the time. Only by being thought about do we learn to think. Some children in some day-care situations get a bit too much training in thoughtlessness.

That said, the two-year-old is interested in other children and very much benefits from playing alongside them and gradually relating more and more to them. If one has a nanny, then it is important to see that the two-year-old also has the benefits of other children's company. Toddler groups – musical groups, library groups, park playground groups – are deservedly popular. They cater to the two-year-old's needs very well: if you are two, you can hang on to the grown-up who brought you if you feel like it but also join in with the action when you're ready.

Parents hardly need telling that the main point, whatever form of care they choose, is to be thoroughly alert and informed about what's going on. This means not only listening to what you're told, but also keeping your powers of observation well to the fore. The most important "thinking minds" that the two-year-old is aware of and depends on will be those of his or her parents. It is those minds that will have to grapple with the difficulties that crop up, as well as the pleasures of the two-year-old's life.

All sorts of care, from the full-time mother to the care of the full-time nursery, can result in a thriving happy two-year-old. But that doesn't mean that "anything goes"; we must expect to feel uncertain about our choice from time to time and even to look back years later and think we wouldn't necessarily do that again. We mostly do our best at the time.

4

The Development of Body and Mind

Play

Play is the two-year-old's work. The child of two plays from the moment he or she wakes up in the morning. Sam could be heard talking to his Peter Rabbit toy even before he came in to see his parents. Peter was his "alter ego", his other self, someone who always kept him company. Yet, of course, Peter didn't really answer back, he remained a charming stuffed toy who, when wound up, played a lullaby. So Sam was on the way to doing without somebody else, on the way to realizing he was alone when he woke up. He was on the way to learning the difference between make-believe and real; he was also thinking about the nature of friendship, and he was certainly experiencing affection towards something a bit less than he was. One can see what a complex variety of functions a few minutes with Peter Rabbit might perform.

A child of two like Sam does not just think in his head. Play is his way of thinking. It is one way of pursuing the child's need to explore both the world of ordinary reality and the world of the mind and the emotions. Sam was playing alone for a few minutes on this occasion, and although it won't last for long at a time, children of this age do practise thinking for themselves on their own at times like this. Daisy's mother overheard her as she squatted in the garden by a small pile of leaves and stones that she was playing with. "Many, many children's gone," she crooned repeatedly. She was concentrating hard. We don't know exactly what was going on in Daisy's mind but she was behaving as though she was considering a matter of real gravity, and something to do with loss.

There is play on your own and play with someone else. The two-year-old is only just starting to grasp the idea of mutual play, and the beginning of this often involves a willing adult or older child. Sam was very much taken by the character of Bob the Builder. He was not alone: this energetic little television person greatly appealed to many small boys. Sam was given a Bob the Builder set, with a yellow hard hat and a plastic set of workman's tools in a carrying-box. When he first saw the helmet, his eyes opened wide, as though he could not have imagined anything so wonderful. To start with, he was shy about putting it on, looking as if he wondered whether or not he was up to such an honour. Sam took to it very quickly though, and played at being Bob the Builder over quite a long period. His mum was required to join in. A character called Wendy was introduced into the programme, and whatever Wendy was like in the original, in his game Sam's mum turned into a Wendy who was not only Bob's helper, but practically his servant, to be told what to do and to do it uncomplainingly.

Sam was playing and thinking what it might be like to be a grown-up man. The first reaction to the wonderful yellow helmet shows how awe-inspiring he feels this man to be. He also makes him lordly, telling Wendy what to do, being grand and powerful with his splendid almost-magic tools. His idea of a grown-up man is of course a little boy's idea; it isn't realiztic. But he is exploring his own ideas and feelings and exploring the world of work and cooperation, all at the level of development that he needs. His mum found his lordly ways sweet and endearing, appropriate to his age, nothing like what they might be if an older child were ordering her about.

Sometimes play is to do with exploring physical possibilities. During the year between the second and the third birthdays children develop greatly. From being still a little unsteady, they acquire more and more mastery of their bodies in running, climbing and riding on things. As with all physical developments, there will be a psychological concomitant. The better you can really do something, the less you have to rely on magic or pretend. Acquiring skills goes beyond the fact that it is indeed essential to be able to run and jump, that the body requires exercise and that physical activity is good for children. It also gives them a feeling of being in charge, properly and rightfully of their own selves.

A great deal of play is to do with acquiring mastery. It is illuminating to think how a child learns to walk, climb and run. It is through incessant practice. Endlessly picking yourself up and trying again goes into it for a good many children. Equally, much imaginative play works on expanding and exercising the mind in the service of developing its muscle. We know that thinking and feeling coexist closely, and there are plenty of ways in which children explore their feelings and learn to think about matters which require effort. It's very common, for instance, for children who have had to go to hospital, or have other medical treatment, to find satisfaction and reassurance in playing with a doctor's pretend medical kit. The hospital situation is one which challenges the child's trust: how can doctors be good and helpful if they hurt you? How can it be that dad or mum joins in and helps the doctor rather than leaps to your defence? This needs explanation, of course; it also needs pure sympathy, but after it's all over there's a place for playing doctors, playing out the explanation, giving Teddy or Peter Rabbit the injection.

Books

We are all encouraged to look at books with our children and to read to them: it's something that most people come to enjoy, and it's interesting to think what a child gets from it. Many two-year-olds already like looking at books and hearing stories, and if they don't yet, then this is a perfect time to start. Although looking at pictures can be an enjoyable solitary occupation, it won't hold a child of this age for long. The experience of sitting with an adult and being read to, however, is somewhat different: there is a warm mutuality to it. It's something you do together with someone else. The two-year-old doesn't just cuddle up against the grown-up's body to read a book: he or she also comes close up to the adult's mind. The adult helps to sustain the child's interest and attention, draws his or her gaze to the pictures and carries the two-year-old along in following the story. The toddler follows an understanding mind along the pathway of the book.

The range of books enjoyed by children of this age can be wide. They still like books for babies – picture books, for example, with realiztic and recognizable versions of things they know in everyday life, and somewhat complicated but similar representations, like a dad cleaning his teeth, a mum on the telephone with a baby on her knee, a toddler in a high chair and so on. Here we have talking points.

Some early books also carry important and relevant messages which give the toddler plenty of food for thought. There are many charming variations on the theme of a "new baby arrives". This theme is relevant even when a new baby *isn't* on the way, because many children between two and three do turn their minds to this question: Alex, the youngest of four and definitely the last in his mother's mind, asked her one day, "When are you having the next baby?" One of the books on this idea is Charlotte Voake's *Ginger*, a cat who had to adapt to the coming of a new kitten. Dogs too are called upon to have their noses put out of joint when a baby is born. The message is they can still be loved, as well as the baby.

Books like this perform the same function as serious art of all kinds does for adults. They open the child's mind to a difficult question and make the idea manageable, provoking further thought. Many books loved by toddlers supplement their everyday experience by introducing them to a vast new range of things, places and ideas. Children will have their own likes and dislikes: one book will speak to one child, one to another. Sam was totally captivated by a book about baby owls whose mother went away and came back. Sarah wanted the story of the three little pigs again and again. Daisy was fascinated by hearing the stories of Rupert Bear even when her mum thought she couldn't really be understanding it all. Books are an important way of feeding the child's natural thirst for knowledge – they aren't the only way, but it seems a waste to ignore them.

Toys and games

Most people are wryly aware that children don't always play with the expensive toys they're given. Many children acquire, in our affluent society, huge quantities of toys. These may well be harmless fun, but they aren't really necessary as a child will always find something to play with. Many two-year-olds will just as soon have a small saucepan and a wooden spoon, or some stones and sticks in the garden, as more elaborate representational toys, but of course parents and grandparents, aunts and uncles all love to give presents and many of them do bring great pleasure.

It's usually the simpler toys, one that have stood the test of time, that give the most lasting enjoyment. Bricks and building cubes, a tea set, cars or trains, soft toys and dolls all provide plenty of opportunity for two-year-olds to exercise their fine motor skills and their thinking capacities.

Imagination and fantasy

We have seen in thinking about play and books how the two-year-old's imagination is active. Sometimes it is almost too active and gets out of control. The two-year-old does not have a firm and corrective grip on reality, and bad dreams or childish fears can at any time in the pre-school years cause much distress. Sarah woke in the night crying inconsolably, clearly dreadfully frightened. Her mother discovered that she was frightened of a carved Victorian wall-bracket, a little antique shelf for holding a vase, that was up on the wall in Sarah's room. By scrutinizing it carefully, Sarah's mother could just about see that it might look like a man's face. Promptly she said, "Nasty old thing, let's take it away," and removed the offending object. It was probably much more appropriate to do this than to try to explain to poor Sarah that there wasn't anything to be frightened of. Naturally, sometimes explorations may be in order, but Sarah's mother felt that she had done the right thing this time, as Sarah said, "Good," and, hiccupping slightly, went back to sleep. One could imagine what happened was that Sarah had a scary dream and woke to find it apparently true – a horrid man was on the wall looking at her.

Children's minds are occupied at times with worries and fears that we don't really know about. It is as well to be able to cast our own minds back (not perhaps as far as two years old, but to four or five) and remember how real childhood fears can be. It is a relief for children when they can begin the process of distinguishing imagination from reality. Even being able to recognize that what happened was a dream is helpful; very small children can't, and experience it as a real event. Daisy woke crying one night: her parents couldn't distinguish what she was saying at first, but in the end she managed to say, "Daddy's eaten all the biscuits." This sounds sweetly trivial, but Daisy was having a dream that mattered a lot about there being nothing left for her. She was sure it was true about Daddy and the biscuits, and needed explanation and reassurance.

Talking and communication

The examples of Sarah and Daisy dreaming show how important the acquisition of language can be. Fears that can be put into words are less threatening; explorations that can be understood relieve anxiety. Of course, there are many wordless ways of communication, and babies make full use of them, but there are some communications for which only words will do, and the toddler's growing power to put things into words greatly increases his or her grip on the world.

The age at which speech is acquired is notorious for varying widely. It is one of the focal points for parental anxiety. One child will be saying words at one year old; another will be into his third year before uttering. Jessica was not an early talker, but she understood things very well and had more language in her head than usually came out, as was shown when she was taken to hospital and had to have a blood test when she was two-and-a-half. She hated the doctor taking the blood, and when he came back later to tell her mother the satisfactory result, the previously rather wordless Jessica burst forth, "No Blood, No Blood! You DOCODILE!" She was able under pressure to produce not only very clear instructions about not doing it again but also a clever combination of "doctor" and "crocodile" to express her idea that the doctor was cruel.

It can even be a mixed blessing to be very articulate at times, as Nathan's mum observed. Nathan was very good at talking, and had spent much time alone with adults who gave him plenty of practice. In the park, Nathan went up to another little boy his age and said, "Hello, my name's Nathan." The other child looked at him unbelievingly. "Hallo," repeated Nathan, "my name's..." but he didn't finish because the other boy, impatient at this small person who was getting in his way, just gave him a bit of a shove and Nathan, crestfallen, fell over. It also happened that people expected him to be more grown-up than he was. However, his mother formulated to herself the idea that although Nathan was verbally sophisticated, even precocious, under the skin he was just as small and babyish as the rest of the children his age – just as vulnerable, just as puzzled by life, just as easily pleased by baby things.

Nathan sometimes tried to push himself to understand difficult concepts, as though he were an adult before his time. All small children live in a world that's a bit beyond them. There are some things that children have to be content to let go, knowing that they can't grasp them yet. Sometimes an event like a bereavement or a divorce happens and has to be explained to a toddler. This is very hard for the parent, who knows that something has to be said but can't think how to do it. Maybe all one can do is to start the communication in the full knowledge that it will have to be returned to later. The death of a grandparent is not so uncommon, and there is no way that a two-year-old is able to conceptualize death straight away. The idea of "gone and never coming back" is too frightening for that.

There are all kinds of topics, sometimes of great importance, which have to be broached in the very simplest terms around this age, with the parent's awareness that it's the work of a long time – years perhaps – to see it assimilated. Such topics include adoption, the absence of a father or a mother, the position of a child with same-sex parents, the death of a parent or sibling. It's no good giving too high a dosage of explanation too soon. The child's anxiety will be raised by something that's overwhelming and you will have the reverse of the effect you want by making questioning harder. Maybe you will achieve the result of getting the child to parrot complicated explanations – that would have been easy with the verbally expert Nathan – without any deep understanding. In this respect, as in all others, it is vital to remember the age of the child, and the fact that its mind is as soft, vulnerable and immature as its body.

Television and videos

Television is quite a different topic, and yet linked. If we are to believe newspaper research, small children of two and three spend a good deal of time in front of the television. Many parents are concerned about this, and feel the need to work out for themselves what's wise and suitable in this respect. What can the two-year-old manage and benefit from?

Maybe it's as well to recall what many children look like while they're watching television. Frequently they are goggling, thumbs in mouth and eyes fixed on the screen. When this is combined with awful shrieks when the set's turned off, as though something that had been glued together were being dragged apart, I think we can take it for granted that not a lot is going on in their heads. They have found a method of filling a gap. Well, one might say, what's the matter with that? Indeed, for short spaces of time it seems fairly harmless. We all use television as a minder for the children occasionally, and as long as they're watching something that isn't going to upset them, it seems a reasonable way to fill a tired gap between tea and bed.

It's illuminating to compare this sort of passive watching with real participation, when a child's interest is aroused and engaged. Or the difference when an adult watches with a child, when the experience can come much closer to that of reading a book. We all have to engage with the television, but how do we convey the need for discrimination – for watching what you actually want to watch? It's almost as though the glued-to-the-screen type of watching were addictive, something that a child can't bear to stop. It may be now that there are so many good videos for small children that video-watching can become rather more like choosing which book you'll reread. That would seem to remove a little of the passivity which led Jessica's dad to say "That child would watch the News in Welsh!" (and let me add they didn't speak Welsh).

There is a different concern, not connected with small children sitting there failing to absorb anything, but on the contrary connected to their absorbing some of the wrong stuff. I am not talking about profoundly unsuitable viewing, such as pornography or adult violence. We know quite well that this does children no good at all. But it is still possible, well below this level of unsuitability, to find things that are fine for older children but not for tinies. This may be another area where it matters if the adults in charge know what's going on.

It sounds old-fashioned to say so, but there really is such a thing as being over-excited. Children can be over-stimulated by programmes that stir them up. Sam become transfixed by a video he had watched with the neighbour's children, asking again and again when he could see it once more, waking in the night with it on his mind. We can see from this that it was simply too strong a mixture for his young system to cope with. At every stage of a child's development it's vital that the child should be his or her age.

The adults in the child's world

Finally, as we think about the two-year-old's developing character, we might glance again at important adults in his or her life, and think about the wider sphere of the family. Grandparents, aunts and uncles, cousins – all these have the advantage that they're not going away; they're different from nannies or teachers on the whole, because they're there, somewhere, forever. As an adolescent girl reluctantly admitted, "Well, I suppose I know that even my least favourite aunt would probably always stick by me."

The toddler has to start the business of making the best of the family he or she has got. Families, of course, can be a curse as well as a blessing sometimes, but it's enlarging and enlivening for the small child when there are significant relationships to be made outside the immediate circle. It's not at all rare for people to be better grandparents than they were parents, for example – they learnt something, after all. They can offer a different perspective and tempo, at best. Young uncles and aunts can be most enthusiastic helpers and babysitters, and the toddler forms real and lasting relationships with them.

5

The Parents

Hard work

This brief chapter acknowledges how complicated and demanding the job of bringing up a two-year-old can be when you take it seriously, and especially when you are not yet experienced. Chapter 4 referred to grandparents who have learnt something: an older mother who has brought up a girl and a boy, both of whom had done well, looked back at these early years somewhat ruefully. She remembered how she had struggled to keep a demanding career and utter commitment to her children going at the same time, and she said that now she felt (and only now) that she could really enjoy just simply looking after small children. "Oh well," she said, "I suppose I was training to be a granny."

This doesn't mean that she didn't have times of great pleasure from her children's company, progress and characters. It does mean that small children are hard to be with twenty-four hours a day. Why is this? It links to another point that it's interesting to consider. What store of experience and knowledge do we draw upon in bringing up our children? There will be a variety of answers to this: some people will say that they helped with younger siblings, babysat as a teenager, have a professional interest, read widely in preparation, or they will say they came to it absolutely free of any previous experience at all that they know of. However true all these may be, there is an additional factor. We have all been two years old. That experience of being a two-year-old is there in ourselves, deep down but influential, as surely as is our experience of being 12 or 22.

This has minuses and pluses. On the minus side is the way in which our ancient two-year-old anxieties are reignited. We know only too well how unbearable it can be to be tiny and weak, and we shy away from it. On the plus side, this is itself an advantage. This is how we understand what it's like to be them. We need to have a hot line to how they feel, but at the same time we must hang on to what we know as adults. The pull between the two produces a tension which is tiring.

Moreover, we bring to the task of being a parent a vast amount of what is often called "baggage". Our children's childhood recalls our own childhood to us – and this is the experience that we draw on, often without realizing it. A person who has been, decades ago, a well-looked-after baby, has quite a good chance of looking after a baby well in her or his turn. When our children arrive at the toddler stage, our own toddler years are re-evoked, ghostly and powerful, out of sight.

Things can go back more than one generation. Daisy and Annie's mother, struggling with the rivalry between two little girls, could not understand why she was making such heavy weather of a toddler and a baby. She remembered some jealousy between her older brother and herself, but not like this. But long ago, her own mother had been one of two girls. The other little girl in the family was just the same age, having been suddenly adopted at the age of two because she was orphaned. Could some difficulty have been passed down unsolved? If everything is smooth, there's nothing to bother about. It's only when parents rub up against anxiety that doesn't pass that extra thinking is needed, and perhaps a look at what experience the parents have brought to the task is valuable. What was your childhood like? What, indeed, was your parents' childhood like?

When to worry

Many parents of small children worry a good deal, on and off, especially with their first child. However, experience brings some confidence in knowing when one should be worrying. Very small children can't manage their own problems, conflicts, fears or anxieties; caring for them still involves not only physical intimacy, but also mental intimacy. We feel with and for them, and we tend to go up and down with them.

What about problems that don't go away? Jasmine was a single parent with a little boy, Joe. Instead of Joe's gaining in independence, he seemed to Jasmine to be getting more and more clingy. It hardly seems right to talk about a two-year-old regressing to babyhood, when they're barely out of it anyway, but Joe seemed determined not to sleep on his own; he often refused meals;

and he showed not the slightest sign of coming out of nappies. He had been in the nursery for some time, and there began to be trouble about saying goodbye in the mornings. It was the final straw when one of the workers at the nursery took Jasmine aside and said Joe was being cross and aggressive with other children.

There is a simple rule of thumb which says, "Look round at all the aspects of a child's life. Is he eating? Sleeping? Getting on with other children? Enjoying himself? Learning new things?" If the disturbance is in only *some* areas like these, it seems reasonable to wait and see, or perhaps to give a little extra special nannying, a touch of back to baby care. For instance, when Simon begged for his bottle in a whiny period after the new baby was born, his parents thought it was better to give it to him wholeheartedly rather than to make a fuss; and to give it with a cuddle, and let him suck sitting on somebody's knee, rather than allowing him to trail dismally about with it. This period in Simon's life showed definite upset; he had trouble sleeping, he refused food on and off – but at the same time there were obvious spurts of development, like an enlargement of vocabulary. This situation comes into the category of temporary disturbance, made more tolerable because it was clear that it was the birth of a new sibling that had shaken Simon up: the source of the trouble was plain. However, Jasmine and Joe were in a different situation. Joe began to be aggressive at home as well as at nursery; he developed tantrums that couldn't be appeased. There was trouble all round. Where did the root lie? Not that there is ever much to be got from thinking "Whose fault is it?" and trying to apportion blame, but there is a great deal to be said for trying to understand a situation that seems at first to be puzzling and meaningless. Jasmine felt that she was immensely unfortunate, struggling to bring up Joe on her own. It seemed the last straw to have such a difficult boy. She had no mother, no sisters at hand. Where could she turn?

She went to her family doctor, who suggested that the health visitor might help. It was clear to the health visitor, a kind and experienced woman, that Jasmine was depressed. Indeed, when Jasmine began to talk and to think about it, she herself saw that this wasn't a new state of affairs; she'd been increasingly low, unhappy, lonely and miserable over the last few months since her partner had finally left her and Joe. It makes sense to think that Joe was reacting strongly to his feeling that something was the matter with Mummy. All his efforts to cheer her up came to nothing. He became sad and depressed, not eating or sleeping well. He got angry and frightened, cross with his mum for not being herself, and scared to be alone or to leave her because he was bothered about her. Also, though Jasmine's relationship with Joe's dad had been difficult, Joe was wondering where his dad had gone.

There was a great deal for Jasmine to think about, and she realized that she had been pushing it to the back of her mind. The health visitor arranged for her to see the counsellor at the medical practice, which proved to be useful: Jasmine had too much to worry about to do it on her own. As she recovered, she was able to think about the sort of relationship she and Joe's dad might manage so that Joe could see his father, and also Jasmine was able to take a fresh interest in people and activities, and get a feeling that her life wasn't over.

Joe picked up remarkably well as his mum became less depressed, renewed her contact with friends and fellow mums and began to wonder if she could take on a job.

Difficulties in the family

As we see from considering Joe's state of mind, two-year-olds often act like a gauge – a sort of barometer or thermometer, reacting to the weather or the temperature of the family. The two-year-old is only just separating himself or herself out as an individual and tends even more than an older child to stand or fall by the family fortunes.

Lucy and Matt decided to make a significant change in their lives. Lucy was offered promotion and a large increase in income if she would accept a job posting to a distant city. Given that property was cheaper there, she and Matt thought that the best thing would be to accept it and for Matt to give up work and take on the household and the care of Ned. But the decision had to be made speedily and the change for them all was enormous, involving not only a significant shift in role for Matt, heavy new work responsibilities and longer hours for Lucy, but also leaving behind all the grandparents who had been such staunch supporters.

The person who on the surface got into the worst state was Ned, who took to clinging to his mother's legs to try to stop her going to work, then screaming inconsolably in a way that Matt found ghastly and unbearable. Then Ned's eczema, which had faded, returned with a vengeance. He fell over at nursery and had to go to hospital with a fearful (though luckily not dangerous) bang on the head. Eventually Lucy and Matt were grimly, quietly quarrelling most of the time they were together; their rows centred on the management of Ned, who became ever more hard to handle.

A painful time was had by all. It started to ease only when Lucy's cousin came to stay and there was the chance for some discussion about the set-up in general, rather than endless grim talk between the parents about "the problem of Ned". To cut a turbulent story short, Lucy and Matt came to see that they'd made something of an unthinking decision: could Matt really bear to be home all day? Did Lucy actually want to be out of the house from seven in the morning till eight at night? Were there, perhaps, some compromises to be negotiated when Matt had finished his renovation work on the house?

Here we have a situation where it looks as though the problem is in Ned, but in fact it lies with the whole family's natural difficulty in grappling with change of such a radical sort. Broadly speaking, two-year-olds are extremely reactive.

Troubles within the toddler

It would be wrong to think that difficulties can never originate in the toddlers themselves. Looking back to Ben, who wanted to tip Ruby off the sofa, it is clear that his jealousy and envy are his own, and nobody else's. He and Danny, who bullied Nathan, might end up in much the same place, though for different reasons. Ben was tempted to attack his sister when his mother was out of the room, and she came back all smiles, saying how good Ben was with Ruby. Equally, Danny's parents' reprovals made Danny attack Nathan secretly. Neither boy had a parent at this time who could be like Jessica's; Jessica startled her mum by displaying aggression towards a younger child who stole her sand-bucket. Jessica's mother, albeit with some discomfort, could tolerate a less good version of Jessica. She could ultimately take a philosophical view, thinking to herself, "the poor child's only human."

Ben's hostile jealousy was ignored and discounted as though it were not a part of him. Danny's attacks on Nathan were regarded as naughty and bad, rather than deserving of understanding. His parents did not see that there is a great deal of difference between naughtiness, where a child has the choice (and can exercise it) between acting one way and acting another; and something more than naughtiness, a kind of disturbance where Danny was impelled from within and *couldn't* simply stop. He needed help – probably help in the form of supervision, where he and Nathan weren't left alone together – and help more generally in the form of understanding that miserable disturbance was inevitable in a child whose family is in turmoil.

Complex family situations

Many toddlers have to master families where there is not so much difficulty as complexity. What, for example, about the toddler who is the newcomer in a reconstituted family, where there may be siblings on both sides from previous relationships? What about toddlers in same-sex partnerships, where the question of "Where did I come from? Who made me?" is a profound one? There are toddlers like Joe whose parents are separated, toddlers who have two sets of parents, toddlers whose parent is single by choice.

Is there anything to worry about here? Can we say anything helpful at all about the new and different shapes families are taking? An important point to remember is that two-year-olds are forging their future identities. This is itself a complicated process, depending not only on what the child sees and is told, but also on what the child *makes* of what happens and of what people say. People have a regard for "conditioning" which can be exaggerated: at times one hears how someone is supposed to behave in a particular way because society, or their parents, or somebody else, enforced it upon them. Maybe. But look at all the occasions when nothing like this has happened. It's reassuring, perhaps, to think that the influence of our parents is limited; that other families, events, people or institutions play their part in shaping children's lives, let alone the part that the child's own individual character plays.

Human beings are both resourceful and adaptable. We need to remember, in all circumstances when we consider small children, how vulnerable and dependent they are. They can never be a grown-up person's helper, let alone partner. Certainly they can be helpful: the most frequent help they give is by being themselves. The lively, developing two-year-old is, at best, the point of hope in a family, a hope that things will go well and perhaps better than in the past.

Conclusion

The third year of childhood shows startling developments. At the beginning of it there is a wide discrepancy between toddlers' levels of attainment. Some are highly accomplished physically, able to run and climb, already showing signs of being fascinated by ball games. Some have polished up their fine motor skills and can concentrate on building blocks or other ways of putting things together. Some are neat and tidy eaters; some are clean and dry by day and even at night; some speak in well-turned sentences and can engage in complicated conversations.

On the other hand, there are toddlers whose legs and arms work with far less confidence and zest, who could no more climb or kick a ball than fly; there are those who show little interest in bricks or constructional toys and games. There are two-year-olds who have no great ambition to feed themselves or who strongly resist the suggestion that it's time to use a potty. And there is the great band of those who can hardly speak at all, although their non-verbal communication skills may be excellent.

By the time the third birthday arrives, the picture is evening out. Walking, talking, toilet-training are all within the compass of the ordinary three-year-old, give or take the odd blip. The three-year-old will have something more of a sense of self, more of the capacity to start thinking about playing with other children who are also conceived of as separate selves. This is a long process, and it is only just beginning: at the start of the third year, just after the second birthday, the two-year-old is still needing to be attached to an older person. In a group setting, whether in day-care or in a social situation, the toddler of two relates primarily to sustaining adults. Gradually the capacity for relationships with children of a similar age begins to grow and by the time the third birthday arrives the earliest friendships begin to be possible. Cooperation, playing together, joining in games are all likely to occur only in a fleeting way, but a process is in train whereby the toddler is developing into a child, who by the age of four or five is able to enjoy some independent relationships as school begins. This ability depends on the child's gradual awareness that other people are individuals who have their feelings, wishes, likes and dislikes; they don't merely exist in relation to the toddler, but as individuals in their own right.

We never entirely outgrow our infant selves; there is always something in us which believes in magic, good and bad, which sees our parents as existing only as our mother and father, not as ordinary human beings without special powers over us. This part of our character, deeply buried or highly active, still feels that we ought to be looked after in a magical way, that all our wants should be supplied, all our troubles eased and all our fears chased away. The two-year-old is born to the human condition where miracles do not happen and magic does not exist, but he or she is only at the start of discovering this.

In one sense it's a disappointment to discover that we aren't in all-powerful control. The two-year-old tries to replicate in the outside world the conviction that he or she is in charge. Often it's hard not to agree with this vigorous belief: everywhere one finds adults tempted to go along with the toddler's conviction that he or she must *not* go to bed, *not* eat what he or she doesn't fancy, *not* allow Mummy and Daddy time alone. The converse has often been the temptation too: the adults' belief that it is dangerous to indulge a toddler's whims. The mature grown-up line can be hard to hold, where we look after the very immature person, help him or her to see that reality is tough but that it is our only salvation. Getting to grips with the idea that you are neither lord of the universe nor a lowly worm is a lifetime's job. Two-year-olds in this year of their lives are forging ahead to learn what they can truly achieve, what actual control they have over themselves and their surroundings; and they are continuing the process of setting the foundations of their grown-up characters.

Further Reading

Bowlby, J. (1979) *The Making and Breaking of Affectional Bonds.* London: Tavistock Publications.

Daws, D. (1989) *Through the Night: Helping Parents and Sleepless Infants.* London: Free Association Books.

Fraiberg, S.H. (1976) *The Magic Years: Understanding the Problems of Early Childhood.* London: Methuen.

Harris, M. (1975) *Thinking about Infants and Young Children.* Strath Tay, Pershire: Clunie Press.

Hindle, D. and Smith, M.V. (eds) (1999) *Personality Development: A Psychoanalytic Perspective.* London and New York: Routledge.

Philips, A. (1999) *Saying "No": Why It's Important for You and your Child.* London: Faber & Faber.

Waddle, M. (2002) *Inside Lives: Psychoanalysis and the Growth of the Personality.* Tavistock Clinic Series. London: Karnac.

Winnicott, D.W. (1964) *The Child, the Family and the Outside World.* London: Penguin.

Helpful Organizations

Exploring Parenthood
Latimer Education Centre
194 Freston Road
London W10 6TT
Tel: 020 8964 1827
Parents' Advice Line: 020 8960 1678

Gingerbread Association for One Parent Families
7 Sovereign Close
London E1W 2HW
Tel: 020 7488 9300
Advice Line: 0800 018 4318
www.gingerbread.org.uk
Support for single parent families

Local SureStart Organisation (in the UK)
SureStart Unit
Dfes and DWP
Level 2, Caxton House
Tothill Street
London SW1H 9NA
Tel: 0870 000 2288
www.surestart.gov.uk

Nursery and Pre-school Information Line
PO Box 5
Brecon
LD3 87X
Tel: 01874 638007

Parentline Plus
Tel: 0808 800 2222 (helpline 24 hours a day)
www.parentlineplus.org.uk
Information and support for parents

PlayMatters/National Association of Toy and Leisure Libraries
68 Churchway
London NW1 1LT
Tel: 020 7255 4600
www.playmatters.co.uk

Pre-school Playgroups Association
61–63 Kings Cross Road
London
WC1 9LL
Tel: 020 7833 0991
www.pre-school.org.uk

Under-fives Counselling Service
The Tavistock Clinic
120 Belsize Lane
London NW3 5BA
Tel: 020 7435 7111
www.tavi-port.org (under Patient Services, Infant Mental Health Service)

YoungMinds/National Association for Child and Family Mental Health
102–108 Clerkenwell Road
London EC1M 5SA
Tel: 020 7336 8445
Parents' Information Service: 0800 018 2138
www.youngminds.org.uk

Index

abusive relationships, effects on children 34
advice and support
  during periods of instability 19
  role of health visitors 49–50
aggressive behaviours 35–7, 49–50, 51
anger, dealing with feelings 17, 24

"battle of wills" 16–18, 54
  dealing with emotional "fallout" 17, 22
  over bedtimes 24–5
  over eating 22–3, 27–8
  over toilet-training 26
bedtimes 23–5
  refusing to go to bed 23
  sharing parental bed 24
books
  for children 41–2
  for parents 55
bossiness 15
boundaries 16–18
  dealing with antisocial behaviours 35–7
  establishing playtime "rules" 36
  value of routines 18–19
  when to say "No" 17
  see also "battle of wills"
bullying behaviours 35–7

challenges and stressful situations
  coping mechanisms 18–19
  see also "battle of wills"
child development
  milestones at two years old 9–10
  milestones at three years old 53–4
  concepts of time and memory 18
  differences between children 11, 27–8

need for stability 18–19
childcare arrangements 37–8
childminders 37
"clingy" behaviours 30, 34, 49
communicating with children, using simple terms 44–5
confidence and reassurance 53–4
  setting boundaries 16–18, 35–7, 53–4
  value of routines 18–19
copying peer behaviours 36

divorce and marital problems 25, 52

emotional development
  dealing with anxieties 27–8
  dealing with feelings of aggression 35–7
  see also child development; exploring and learning
emotions
  feeling angry with children 17, 24
  "ups" and "downs" 15–16
exhaustion, recognising toddler tiredness 16
exploring and learning
  stages of understanding 13–14
  through books and storytelling 41–2
  through extended social networks 46
  through play 34–5, 39–41, 42
  through talking and language 43–5
  through videos and television 45–6
Exploring Parenthood 57

families 46
  being an only child 34–5
  complex relationships 52
  coping with changes and difficult times 19
  sibling relationships 36–7, 31–4
father–child relationships 30–1
  support roles 32–3
feeding patterns

learning to self-feed 22, 27–8
likes and dislikes 22
friendships
  and bullying behaviours 35–7
  copying peer behaviours 36
  difficulties for "only" children 34–5

genetic make-up 13
Ginger (Voakes) 42
Gingerbread Association for One Parent
  Families 57
grandparents 46

health visitors, role in supporting
  families 49–50

imagination and fantasies 39–40, 42–3
independence 53–4
  at two years old 9–10
  at three years old 53–4
  learning to self-feed 22
  see also exploring and learning
information sources
  books for parents 55
  helpful organizations 57–8
inherited characteristics 13

jealousy
  of mother–father relationships 30–1
  when a new baby arrives 32–3

language
  "No" – a two-year-old's favourite
    word 16–17
  and understanding 43–5
  using age-appropriate words 44–5
loneliness, at bedtimes 23–4

memory 18
milestones at two years old 9–10
milestones at three years old 53–4

mother–child relationships 30
moving jobs/houses 50

nannies 37–8
naughtiness
  and aggressive behaviours 35–7,
    49–50, 51
  and childhood disturbances 51
  reverting back to "baby" behaviours
    33, 49
  understanding "motivations" 35–7,
    49, 51
nightmares 23–4, 43
"No", as favourite word 16, 26
nurseries 37–8
Nursery and Pre-school Information
  Line 57

"only" children, difficulties approaching
  peers 34–5
"over-excitement" 16, 46

parent–child "battles" *see* "battle of
  wills"
parental reactions, toddler tantrums and
  "demands" 17, 24, 47–8
parental relationship difficulties 25, 52
parenting 47–8
  coping with family difficulties 50–1
  dealing with feelings of anger 17, 24,
    47–8
  dealing with own feelings/childhood
    experiences 48
  when to bring in outside help 48–50
Parentline Plus 57
play 39–43
  learning to be with other children
    34–7
  using imagination and fantasy 42–3
playgroups 37–8
PlayMatters 58
Pre-school Playgroups Association 58

pregnancy, coping with older children's feelings 31–4

reading to children 41–2
rivalry 33
routines, value to children 18–19

safety issues, toddler-proofing the home 17–18
same-sex parents 52
saying "No"
  a two-year-old's favourite word 16
  when to set limits 17
  see also boundaries
separations
  at bedtime 23–5
  and family stressful situations 50–1
  feeling excluded from parental relationships 31
siblings
  aggressive behaviours 36–7
  coping when a new baby arrives 31–4
single parents 48–50, 52
  when to seek outside help 49–50
sleep patterns 23–5
step-children 52
story-telling 41–2
SureStart 57

talking
  different abilities 43–4
  parental expectations 44
  using simple terms 44–5
tantrums 17, 49
  see also "battle of wills'
telephones 14
television 45–6
time, lack of concept 18
toddler groups 38
toilet-training 25–6
toy libraries 58

toys 42
  using imagination and fantasy 42–3

Under-fives Counselling Service 58

videos 45–6
  and over-stimulation 46

Young Minds 58